THE SIMPLE SCIENCE OF CREATING LASTING CHANGE

THE SIMPLE SCIENCE OF CREATING LASTING CHANGE

FINNEGAN JONES

CONTENTS

1 Introduction to Micro Habits — 1
2 Psychological and Behavioral Theories — 5
3 The Impact of Micro Habits on Daily Life — 9
4 Practical Strategies for Implementing Micro Habits — 13
5 Measuring and Tracking Progress — 17
6 Case Studies and Success Stories — 21
7 Challenges and Obstacles in Sustaining Micro Habit — 25
8 Future Directions and Research Opportunities — 29

Copyright © 2024 by Finnegan Jones
All rights reserved. No part of this book may be reproduced in any manner whatsoever without written permission except in the case of brief quotations embodied in critical articles and reviews.
First Printing, 2024

CHAPTER 1

Introduction to Micro Habits

What I've noted is that most people have discovered independently that their improved habits often did have a micro habit. While correlation doesn't prove causation, the sheer number of times people have independently referred to micro habits – whether I noticed it directly or found it in other people's material – is an encouraging point. The real potency of micro habits comes from being able to successfully introduce small changes into life so that they scale up to become unconscious habits with less investment of time and energy than standard habits."

"In many ways, our lives are shaped by the habits we develop. While our habits may begin with a conscious decision or non-decision, they become almost entirely unconscious over time. For individuals who hope to make change happen, they need to figure out a way to interrupt existing habits and introduce new ones. The micro habit is a small routine that occurs consciously and is designed to form an unconscious habit. Because only one micro habit is focused on at the beginning of the change process, it requires less willpower to activate the habit over time. This is a marked change from the old view of changing habits, which said that change must occur in a specific and inflexible pattern: 1. Make it a habit that requires willpower, 2. Maintain it as an investment, and 3. Form it over time.

Definition and Conceptual Framework
Micro habits exist primarily to form a durable, episodic behavior change when you want to form a habit specifically in a targeted behavior you don't already do. They should be performed only in a specific context, during which time it becomes second nature for several reasons that relate closely with the topic of this book. Context can be the time of day or location but should attempt to define what it is specifically about that context that triggers the behavior. Micro habits are not intended to build a new habit into your current daily routines nor to cultivate short-term situational dependences (so-called "episodic habit"). You can form a micro habit only if that habit is not already established, and that micro habit should be dropped when the behavior is autonomous and no longer needs reinforcement.

Micro habits then are like a pet training sequence when a pet is supposed to follow a simple command or demands but currently balks doing so. In the future she/he will perform this without any coaxing. You want to train the pet to take small steps toward the ultimate goal, such as demanding things in a low-distraction environment. Micro habits should be one small "chunk" of the habit you want to develop, performed in an environment that makes it easy to remember, and follow with an obvious reward. The ultimate goal is to create a mental link between a situation and Outlook stimulated by autonomous behavioral changes associated with simple-to-perform routine habits, and reinforced by intrinsic rewards for successfully completed behavior.

Your Micro Habit in Your Context Now that you have an understanding of what micro habits are and why you might require one, let's answer the first question: what should your micro habit look like in your specific context? The goal of setting up your micro habit is to create the antecedents for performing the behavior you want through repetition and learning, which can then be followed by cues for spontaneous autonomous behavior. An optimal micro habit is simple, routine, mechanical with a "must do" attitude, habit as shaped by intrinsic motivation to form a memory association directly between the context and behavior. And it officially strategies preference for the Packer et al. analysis (2019).

Historical Background

The simple science of creating lasting change: A study of micro habits. For nearly a decade now, I have been spending time studying micro habits with my clients. I had watched our company's experiments slowly be translated into working versions of my programming, and today I am happy to announce the science that can test the reliability and predictability of micro habits. No promises of overnight transformations; instead, success through well-understood, well-tested principles. Building micro habits by taking very small steps toward encoding a habit repeatedly for eventual automaticity and squashing self-imposed obstacles to habit formation.

As I described my company's work more and more, others responded positively, and I was asked to share it with more and more people. The more steps towards "someday" that we share, the more people who can reach "someday." It was clear to me that behavior recognition programming had the potential to be of help to many more people than just my clients and that the results realized through micro habits could be articulated more clearly.

CHAPTER 2

Psychological and Behavioral Theories

This article is about how taking small steps can increase individuals' likelihood of making big changes. By pointing to psychological and behavior change theories, social science evidence, and literary examples, we seek to explain a basic phenomenon of life: the role of micro habits in personal change and development. We use the term micro habit as a point to focus on the small successes that produce habits which build toward larger goals, allowing readers to find quick initial steps toward making bigger changes towards their better selves. It is our perspective that finding the best way to make these first small transformations can reverse negative trends by reminding us adults and adolescents alike that small decisions can lead to beneficial habits and expounding on research and theory which remind us that habit-formation success is within reach.

The Expectancy-Value Model says people will initiate a behavioral change based on their expectations whether they think they can change and what they think will happen when it does change and the value they place on the results associated with making that change. Researchers have tested and applied this model, more recently in a 2020 article on leisure-time physical activity, like lifetime wellness, finding that perceived physical activity capability was the most significant of the barriers to take-up. If someone does not think that they are capable of being athletic, the benefits of taking the time and effort to learn are not high.

Habit Formation Theories

According to the legislation view (Lewin, 1952), drive reduction is considered the basis for the formation of a habit. First of all, the individual is assumed to have a drive, which tends to cause a behavior that leads to a goal and the reduction of the drive. According to this perspective, habits should be considered as responses, first to drives by goal satisfaction, and only secondarily as an established tendency to act in a given situation (Schein, 1950). According to the reinforcement view, habits are considered as the second stage and stabilization of response. The habit-formation mechanism, the laws of effect and combination of reactions with problems, were studied as forerunners of the principle of reinforcement that eventually resulted in Skinner's theory of learning and compliant behavior through shaping.

Non-reinforcement through learning theory. A typical example of exploring the effects of non-enforcement was the urea experiment. This experiment indicated that, by means of non-reinforcement, there was a decrease in the responses for all 6 levels of reinforcement. This dynamic aspect of behavior, against the context of the interaction with the object of behavior, showed a rapid increase of responses for that level 5-10.

Behavioral Change Models

In classic behavioral change models, change occurs through several major stages. Stages range from precontemplation, when the individual has little awareness or interest in the issue, to contemplation, when the individual starts having ambivalent feelings, to preparation, action, and then maintenance. This model arises from several principles, including consciousness raising (manipulating the amount of information or consciousness of the issue, emotionally creating a realization), decisional balance (weighing the pros and cons of changing behavior), and self-efficacy (confidence in one's ability to cope with high-risk situations without relapse). These issues are manipulated in models like the transtheoretical model (TTM). Unfortunately, this model fails to predict change better than chance in habitual bad behaviors, showing that information is not the bottleneck to change, although it is often used as such.

Many 'change' programs focus on cascading steps like using aids to resolve state (symptoms) behavior and believed, unrealistically, that increased information would lead to change. These programs also did not work for cognition (beliefs), which most people already knew, yet failed to act on. The real bottleneck to change was in the repertories (skills) assumed to maintain habits. Manuals with detailed, complex plans depersonalize the person, beyond the capabilities of people, assuming detailed knowledge. The true determinant of success, repertory, is shown to be the difficulty of habit termination. Individuals need to be trained to become more self-aware, conceptually capable learners who can train themselves, confident generalizers and repertory teachers, capable of deep, dynamic, self-directed learning, like those who self-manage a problem. It stands to reason that then making change is an instinct.

CHAPTER 3

The Impact of Micro Habits on Daily Life

In order to clarify how these ten categories of micro habits simplified my life, I will describe each of them below. To briefly introduce each category, I will state the area or purpose of these micro habits. Some of them I use daily, while others I use less often, but they definitely simplify my life when I use them. These are all micro habits because they are small and automatic. I often do not need to consciously decide to do them, and in many cases, I perform them without being aware of it at all. With the conscious work upfront in creating them, it is now effortless. First, I'll cover ocular micro habits, which are relatively instantaneous and affect the quality of my visual environment.

5.1. Ocular Micro Habits: See Clearly and Relax with Vision Seeing clearly and relaxing my vision. Seeking models to stretch or relax my focus. Reinforcing good habits with nearsight lens use. Shading my eyes and filtering the light. Consciously using my peripheral vision when appropriate.

5.2. Auditory Micro Habits: Relish Beautiful Sounds and Supplement Auditory Malnourishment Enjoying nice tones and sounds. Listen actively, as if you were being recorded. Stopping the very loud.

5.3. Oral Micro Habits: Freshen Breath and Relax with Chocolatey Toothpaste Using toothpaste with pleasant flavors. Refreshing the breath.

5.4. Hair Micro Habits: Detail the Skin Bottleneck with Patient Conditioning Fading Ingrown Hairs Condition and detangle the hair body. Outmaneuver the skin follicle of hair with good timing and technique to minimize discomfort, skin blemishing, and inflammation.

5.5. Sleepwear Micro Habits: Relax Body and Mind with a Minimalist Revolution Layering Solution Using a consistent and sensible minimalist sleepwear system. Providing a reliable, quickly available, noncommittal, controlled temperature environment.

5.6. Pain Management Micro Habits: Apply Topical Analgesics When It Hurts Targeting potential pain sites proactively where it is easy and safe with fast-acting, low-variability-off-target-effect actives using micro wipe application.

Health and Wellness

There's a force in all of us that compels us to form routines and habits, otherwise known as getting stuck in a rut. We all have different types of habits, healthy habits, and not-so-healthy habits. However, the ones that provide instant gratification help to break up the monotony of our day and get our dopamine levels sky high. These are the hardest to break. This is how we create for ourselves these interwoven parallels in our lives. We know the things that currently serve us and give us purpose. We hold them up like a mirror of accountability. Molded and perfected by the days, weeks, months, and even years of repetition.

Our not-so-desirable habits, the ones we work so tirelessly to change, also have the same characteristic. We contract into defined roles of behaviors and then enhance them through repetition, creating these structures and patterns to your everyday behavior. Think for a moment and ask yourself, how much of my day is structured on automatic pilot, with my pattern of behaviors creating my sense of self? Like the mechanism of an automatic tape measure, we spring back to old habits, or we get philosophical about how cheap it is to buy new tapes. I fell into the habit of never changing. We need to take these thoughts out of the repeat cycle. If I always do exactly what I did, and there is no change, then I'm never shaken enough to grow and change.

Productivity and Time Management

The Pomodoro Technique is a time management method developed by Francesco Cirillo in the late 1980s. The technique uses a timer to break down work into intervals, traditionally 25 minutes in length, separated by short breaks. Each interval is known as a Pomodoro, from the Italian word for 'tomato', after the tomato-shaped kitchen timer that Cirillo used as a university student. There are six steps in the original technique: decide on the task to be done, set the Pomodoro (timer) to 25 minutes, work on the task until the timer rings, take a short break (3-5 minutes), after every four Pomodoros take a longer break (15-30 minutes).

This technique is super helpful when really focusing on something. It also ensures that you are taking regular breaks, and the 25/5 split is actually the upper limit for most people when it comes to maintaining focus. Preferred maximum time to work for all most productive people is twenty minutes, with a three to five-minute break. The typical timeframes for a Pomodoro are 25/5, then 25/5, 25/5, 25/5, and then 15 minutes. The Pomodoro technique has the advantage of giving clear demarcation points for tasks. This makes tasks less intimidating, and provides the satisfaction of completing tasks.

CHAPTER 4

Practical Strategies for Implementing Micro Habits

Despite the evidence that micro habits are one of the most effective ways to create lasting change, people often express doubts over their potential. I believe this skepticism is the result of three errors of understanding. In this section, I will address those three errors and offer some practical strategies for how you can implement micro habits in your life.

Error of Time Perspective - The first key error is one of time perspective. When you think of the words "habit" and "routine," you think of long time periods, usually months or years. Another word related to habits is "discipline," which conjures up willpower and huge amounts of effort. Because of this, the type of action associated with these words is also broad in scope. Compound any of these words with the prefix "micro," and those nice, safe concepts of time, effort, and scope aren't so certain anymore. This is the mental hurdle. The laws of physics apply so clearly to our thoughts and actions. If you apply a small amount of force for every block of time, why shouldn't energy and effort compound in the way that works best for us? All that glitters is not gold. Our brains can only handle such a weighted average over a forced period of time. Practice doesn't really make "perfect" (but "practice" (a period of time after which the possibility of failure or misunderstanding arises) does. The biggest step towards overcoming this error is to take the long-term perspective of assistance.

Setting Clear Goals

A first step in creating change in your life is to set a clear goal. By setting a goal, you are focused on an endpoint and a clear target. You are taking a step towards overcoming indecisiveness – you are no longer trying to decide what to focus on because you have already decided where you want to finish. Having a goal means that you can make decisions based on how well they do or do not support your overall aim. By being specific about what you want, you are creating a check and balance system that works to keep you in line with your intentions. It is much easier to waver when you are flexible, so by setting a goal, you are making it much harder to "change your mind." You are in control, and that is the most powerful state any of us can be in. Would a train ever reach its destination if it didn't have a set of tracks to follow? Your goal is your track into the future – it's the path you need to take if you're going to get to where you want to end up.

Remember, I'm not asking you to completely define your goal today or this week. What I am asking you to do is to think long and hard about what you want to achieve over the next 30 days, one and two years. We'll work on short-term goals first as these are the most important, but for now, I want you to set a longer-term goal so that you have a rough idea of the direction you are heading in. The clearer you are in your intentions, then the simpler it will be to make that happen. Think about how you can simplify your life over the long term. Does your big goal really resonate with you? Are you making changes in your life because you really want to, or because you think you should?

Creating a Routine

The process of creating a routine involves chaining an action with an existing well-established habit. You need to start small and then gradually increase the association between the routine and a reward. Over time, the pre-existing habit starts to make the routine seem more automatic. For example, you might want to meditate right after you wake up. Meditation is difficult and boring at first. However, if you add it to your coffee habit or your shower habit, it will not take too long before it feels weird if you don't do your waking minute meditation. Compare the difference between being sick and not being sick. When you're sick, the routine associated with getting ready in the morning feels strange. You're bored and mentally ready to move beyond that routine.

Another example would be listening to a meditative melody before working out. It becomes easier to control signaling thoughts like "it's too hard," "you're tired," and "this is too much" when you know that you need half a zen moment right after. Creating a routine is like watering a sapling that eventually grows into a larger plant. First, you have to notice and identify the positive results that begin to come from the habit. For example, after the introduction and the first meditation, setting a theme for the meditation became more and more important. Higher self-esteem came a month or two later, right after the period where meditation removed most identifying chains. First you grow the self-esteem, then the serenity and the contentment. At first, the process feels alien and forced, letting yourself feel uncomfortable after being uncomfortable-proofed. In order to continue, you constantly have to compare what you were like before with how you feel right now.

CHAPTER 5

Measuring and Tracking Progress

Measuring and tracking progress is an essential part of changing any behavior. The simple act of keeping track of an activity and a corresponding measurement will increase our cognition around that activity. There is plenty of anecdotal evidence for this. Even something as simple as jotting down your food intake for the day can be very informative and can help change eating patterns. Tracking is thinking about the activity.

Tracking provides another essential feature: consistency. Forcing yourself to measure and track an activity forces you to become consistent around that activity. For many types of measurement, consistency can often be more impressive than the measurement itself. Other times, measurement can actually show consistency itself. Both of these concepts are mutually beneficial and create a positive feedback cycle.

For most habits, tracking is a passive but supportive part. Habits have their structure built over a long time, and we are only initiating a series of small changes. The ideal situation is that the final habits will eventually hold themselves and become automatic and thus self-supporting. In a sense, the habits become a part of the structure itself. With the help of the hive mind, we can create a sustainable tracking system. Once we increase our collective behavior measurement consciousness, we can model a better goal setting and feedback system to remain consistent while striving for continuous improvement.

Quantitative vs. Qualitative Measures

Behavior change experiments in digital health systems often rely upon large-scale A/B testing - exposing groups to different versions of systems. Unobtrusive methods are used where systems record user data such as interactions or usage rather than explicitly asking users via questionnaires. However, analyzing the impact of interventions on behavior using unobtrusive methods may lack insights into participants' emotional shifts, values, or secondary effects that participants experienced. On the other hand, designs often gather qualitative data through questionnaires or interviews, and call for qualitative discussions to understand participant experiences.

In pursuing digital behavior change work, striking a balance between qualitative understanding of user experiences and the extraction of quantitative insight may benefit from insights into human behavior derived from other research. We depart from the analysis of behavior change interventions themselves to investigate what insights from the field of psychology can be used. This chapter unpacks psychological concepts that are of interest to any digital behavior change designers for leveraging richer insights quantitatively. We illustrate the potential of the concepts using micro habits, where we could collect data on both the daily behaviors of users and their responses to digital interventions designed to change such behaviors.

Technology and Tools for Monitoring

With recent developments, technology can now help in maintaining diaries of the conduct and habits of people over long periods of time. Diaries that are handwritten, though valuable, are likely to be maintained with a high degree of diligence for only a short period of time. This technology makes it possible for a long array of everyday behavior with coded diaries that are very accurate and useful. Two main advantages of coded diaries over the existing methods are that: a) recall biases/problems associated with asking people questions about their personal lives can be avoided due to the fact that behavioral information is entered in real time, and b) data entry/coding is not necessary. Presently, most methods for monitoring people's habits in real time use audio, video, or diaries to observe a wide set of public health for a short period of time.

In this chapter, we discuss various tools to monitor behavior in real time over long periods. The intent of this chapter is to sensitize technology professionals to the fact that technology can provide users a way of conducting timely tests of relevance and accuracy in the real world and to download up-to-date results instantly, surely, accurately, and in real time mode on related issues that are of interest to researchers. Devices for making long-term studies of day-to-day events, in real time mode, affordably, are likely to be commercially profitable for most of the technology professionals.

CHAPTER 6

Case Studies and Success Stories

The final phase of the research involved an examination of case studies of personal change and self-improvement. I base this analysis on hundreds of testimonials from individuals who report that their lives have been materially changed through nothing more than incredibly minor behavioral adjustments - small steps that are scaled so far down that they take almost no time, require no effort, and demand virtually no interruption or intrusion into their everyday routine. In other words, the only things that seem to work in self-improvement are micro habits.

This phase of the research promises to up his look into the data of observed behavior that constitute the phenomenological landscape of our daily reality. Because, clearly, the only place that behavioral change can take place is in the reality of everyday life. And the human observations, enlightenment, and inspiration that come from this step are nothing less than shocking. The results not only validate the conceptual hypothesis; they destroy every model, idea, and practice ever put forth in the business of personal development and all any qualitative management thinking concerning the business of communication and marketing aimed at personal change. Hence, the conclusions section of this paper is a condensed 20-item statement of the very grossest of my observations.

Individuals

Characteristics of individual agents discussed in the personal strategy literature can be usefully broken out into three categories: motives, cognitive abilities, and learning propensity. Motives are the beliefs and values which cause an individual to act. The strongest influences come not from sophistication or philosopher-kings, but from individuals' interests, worldviews, and fundamental belief systems. These "deep" sources of motivation are a main focus of reality and the recovery myth, and are often resistant to change by policy instruments. More "superficial" motives, such as economic self-interest, social identity, and other-regarding preferences are capable of responding to changes in the policy environment, and are of more immediate concern to the personal strategy literature. Although it is possible to affect the behaviors of individuals who suffer from a lack of cognitive abilities using information or superior expertise, it is not always tempting to do so. Attempts to affect individuals through manipulating learning propensity are more successful.

The literature on personal strategy often talks of "bounded rationality" when referring to the cognitive limitations of individual agents. More nuanced interpretations would be that it is bounded information-processing abilities that plausibly shape these situations, manifested in both knowledge and attention constraints. It is the latter, attention constraints, which are the main focus of this strand of the literature. Here, shortcomings largely originate from a lack of cognitive control rather than a lack of competence, with manipulations to the environment sometimes leading to their short-term remediation. Indeed, in the long run, individual cognitive limitations can be beneficial to the agents that exhibit them: moral and self-improvement require our cognitive fallibility, as an omniscient agent has no real opportunity to choose between vice and virtue. Our boundedly rational agents bear the costs of their actions and attempt to learn and change in response. The more cognitive constraints individuals have, the more effective norm-enforcing social institutions are.

Organizations
Now let's scale up from the individual to discuss how the insights in this book can be applied by organizations. A high level of organizational performance is, in part, the result of productive individual behavior. The elapsed time between an incentive being applied and a desirable behavioral response is a function of both genetic factors and learned preferences. In the education area, it is widely accepted in educational practice that the earlier behavioral inhibitors in life are corrected, the better. However, it has sometimes been difficult to leverage these insights.

However, now that we are coming to understand micro habits, it is possible for managers to tackle productivity problems by implementing the knowledge, skills, and ideas in their organization. Excessive time lags between learning in society and its application in the workplace can compromise economic performance. The production function for innovation in well-resourced societies requires a set of agents starting with individuals with the right mix of scientific and technical knowledge, inventiveness, appropriable skills, curiosity, and an attitude to take well-calculated risks. The environment in which they work must be able to leverage these traits; it must have an effective institutional structure.

CHAPTER 7

Challenges and Obstacles in Sustaining Micro Habit

Like any other new ecosystem, a micro habit system also encounters and has to cross a lot of challenges and obstacles. They could be intrinsic as well as extrinsic. Theoretically, anything beyond our control or influence, be it a situation, people, circumstances or anything else in surroundings can be called an obstacle. That being said, there are a lot of such intrinsic and extrinsic elements that are inherently there with us, as a part of our being. They actively and instantly take some actions just as soon we come across any change, specially, that is against and out of routine.

Some of these are the cognitive dissonance that the change brings about in our minds, the negative and scary voice of our inner lizard, the overrated rational thinking of ours and a few others. Carefully and consciously recognizing and analyzing these challenges will help us in eliminating and neutralizing some toxins that these create in our system. Implemented equally consciously and wholeheartedly, replacing the toxic waste with the curiosity and an open mind will immensely empower and embolden the new young ones to march ahead and taste the success eventually.

Motivation and Willpower

If you're an entirely different person when you go home at night than you are at work, you are not in business completely. And it turns out that this process of turning on and off your motivations and warnings is kind of usually wrecking your life because it's exhausting. And willpower has been found out to be a pretty shameful depletable. The more we use it, the less we have. So a study was done that comes to the participants one at a time into a room and they'd handed them either a plate of freshly baked cookies or a big bowl full of radishes. And they asked them, please sit there in this room with this sweet plate in front of you or this bowl filled with radishes, and between now and the next experiment in 20 minutes, you do not eat the cookies. And as for the radishes, people that were given a plate of cookies did not eat the radish but they sat there and watched the cookies for 20 minutes and then when they came to the next experiment, they cared about the problems and solved the visa.

Research and irritation were all-time high. They'll give up faster than the people who watch the radishes. And any fact of trying to keep suppressing the desire to eat the cookies or the battle, took something out of them that they didn't have her strength. When you try to suppress the cookie thought, and what this tells me is that the metabolic needs are the short-term goals do compete with long-term values about fitness and health. But willpower is not an absent thing. People really were given the highest for challenges in their task-related of the white suppression was lower by 16%. Their relationship might be less satisfying, their second-degree 62% less liking the law-resistant people that didn't have to worry by at least that they also have less willpower and their self-control is destroyed. You're not a different person when you go home and work and home. And the energy and these are two different factors, physical energy and opportunity that are significant motivators and that there are just opportunities in our environment that can either decrease or increase these motivators.

Environmental Factors

After looking at lifestyle attributes such as exercise, diet, and maintaining a healthy weight, individuals seeking to improve their health will also need to recognize certain environmental factors that may be causing poor health and hindering any effects from behavioral changes. These are often things that we have control over, but we may simply not be aware of how they are affecting our health. In cities, people are exposed to large amounts of noise and air pollution, and tend to spend more time in busier environments where violent crimes are more likely to occur. A sudden move to the city may cause further stress that limits the effectiveness of your lifestyle changes. If concerns about your health are a priority, be sure to put as much effort into maintaining your healthy environment as you do your body. Trail-running and hiking may take more time, effort, or money, but you may find that the escape into a beautiful, serene environment provides added benefits.

The word 'habitat' reminds us that where we live does indeed have a huge impact on our health. It is not just our personal habitat, or our work habitat, but also our social and cultural habitats, with whom we live and interact, that define who we are and how we are perceived within our environment. Negative experiences within our various habitats may undeniably stifle how we simply view ourselves and how we interact with the world. Work and life stress management through exposure to natural/environmental habitats has been the topic of a number of other conversations you might find here in these archives. We need the support of our inner and outer-world habitats to be able to fully achieve our potential. Our health is only as good as our environment allows it to be.

Undergraduate college students are at an age where they have much control over their own behaviors, but limited control over their environment due to the requirement to live in undergraduate housing. This limited control makes it especially important that colleges and universities offer a healthy environment for their students. However, restrictive policies sometimes discourage physical activity among undergraduate students. These are policies that at first glance may seem unrelated to exercise behavior, such as requiring full course loads or controlling the availability of and monitor the use of outside equipment. Such policies need to be relaxed in order to help freshmen adjust to college life, or they may already be bringing with them characteristics that make them less likely to be interested in physical activities, such as engaging in sports.

CHAPTER 8

Future Directions and Research Opportunities

What are the big ideas in psychology and decision making consistent with this hypothesized path for approaching change through micro habits? Does creating change one micro habit at a time fit within known processes in the brain that enable the development of knowledge structures? And, does the frequency and spacing of micro habit practice promote neural processes that enable an individual's ability to enhance personal competence over time as hypothesized?

From numerous research programs in the "big ideas" in psychology and related areas, we've learned a great deal over time. But so far, much of this necessarily was accomplished by examining "how" within constraints, limitations and inflexibility of examining "all of it". In part, there is a disconnect - a sometimes disengagement, even schism from examinations of "how". Efforts promoted by small ideas in contrast are more often autonomously related to enhancing personal growth and competence. Once the connections and more complex pathways of influence are understood from the small ideas, will macro ideas provide corroboration and celebrate these ideas on a bigger inclusive stage? Theory-driven research focused on a specific step within this hypothesized linkage from small to macro leading to a multidirectional kind of convergence late in the course of personal growth would be most welcome. At the same time, carefully nurtured, we believe the efforts will lead to thinking forward about the place of macro ideas in informing improvements in how all general goals of developing personal competence, creativity, equipoise, and individual as well as collective happiness in the most effective manner.

Emerging Trends in Behavior Change

In the past decade, behavioral scientists have been developing well-researched strategies that engage a broader range of intervention models. These include: motivating and enabling validated strategies; features that support attention, memory, and decision making; design and individual tailoring for engagement; and options for continuous, multi-player support. Most healthcare professionals (HCPs) look for ways to improve patient health behaviors and seem to be willing to employ evidence-based strategies when we are taught about them and have the means, such as easy-to-implement tools. It is important to meet these behavioral requirements with programmed tools, which can be increasingly integrated into healthcare delivery. Crucially, the tools and strategies we populate them with not only integrate evidence-based strategies for health behavior that have shown efficacy but also can be personalized and designed with the user.

Interdisciplinary Perspectives

Over the years, many self-help books have been written. Psychologists have traditionally been among the most prolific contributors; in recent years, we have been joined by behavior therapists, psychiatrists, and counseling professionals who seek to communicate their views on a larger platform. Others have struck a balance, using interdisciplinary knowledge to develop behavior change strategies and interventions in fields such as natural resource management, health, environmental education, and business. Substantial progress on a keystones goal of behavior change intervention, reducing high-risk behaviors, is taking place in such fields as healthy behavior, maturity onset diabetes, and congestive heart disease. It seems that at least some core knowledge of success across a variety of fields exists. If this knowledge were brought together in one place, some chance for dissemination could exist.

www.ingramcontent.com/pod-product-compliance
Lightning Source LLC
LaVergne TN
LVHW092102060526
838201LV00047B/1522